And Yet . . .

And Yet . . .

A Faith Journey

Pedro. A. Sandín-Fremaint

Foreword by Carter Heyward

RESOURCE *Publications* · Eugene, Oregon

AND YET . . .
A Faith Journey

Resource Publications
An Imprint of Wipf and Stock Publishers
199 W. 8th Ave., Suite 3
Eugene, OR 97401

www.wipfandstock.com

PAPERBACK ISBN: 978-1-6667-3036-4
HARDCOVER ISBN: 978-1-6667-2177-5
EBOOK ISBN: 978-1-6667-2178-2

SEPTEMBER 7, 2021

For Annie

"This is how it always is when I finish a poem.

A great silence overcomes me, and I wonder

why I ever thought to use language."
—RUMI

"History could make a stone weep."
—MARILYNNE ROBINSON

CONTENTS

FOREWORD

IN THESE PROSE-POEM presentations, Pedro A. Sandín-Fremaint dives deeply into the core of mystery which he believes (and thinks) is divine/God. As before, in *The Holy Gospel of Uncertainty* (2017), he is motivated by strong currents, sometimes merging, sometimes crashing, of faith and doubt, relentless gratitude and holy rage.

Throughout this brief volume, the man who emerges from the dive is bound to be related, at least spiritually if not genealogically, to saints of old who refused to make peace with oppressive theologies, silly spiritualities, or false creeds.

The Pedro we meet in the pages of *And Yet* . . . is a man seeking truth, which he knows at the outset is not an immovable "thing," much less, contrary to what he learned as a Catholic boy, a set of doctrines.

There are moments here when I'm reminded of Elie Wiesel's confession that, at last, he prayed to the God in whom he no longer believed. Like Wiesel, Sandín-Fremaint finds something compelling, and probably sacred, in the questions themselves. "Will it ever be possible to construct a world of universal compassion, kindness, and tenderness? How would meaning be arbitrated in such a world?" (53)

Knowing what we know, unable to pretend not to have seen what we too have seen, it is impossible not to weep in the tender encounter of the hope that sparkles in the eyes of Pedro's grandson with the "searing image of another boy whose body lolls on an unwelcoming beach"? (11)

Like Sandín-Fremaint, this reader also asks the "little weed" a question: "how do you hold despair at bay?" (10) I believe Pedro's answer to his own question is to write poetry and prose, to write words chosen and chiseled with care.

I suspect, or maybe I am just projecting, that, for Pedro, to write is to pray, which is why *And Yet...* is in truth a prayer book. This is a splendid collection, a precious gift to me as a sister seeker of honesty, compassion, and sacred truth.

REV. CARTER HEYWARD, PhD
Brevard, North Carolina

ACKNOWLEDGEMENTS

TWO YEARS AGO, I was part of a wonderful group at the Unitarian Universalists of Transylvania County in Brevard, North Carolina, that met biweekly under the name *The Joy of Being*. It was there that this book began to germinate in my mind and heart. My deepest gratitude to Sandy Jones, Christine Schmidt, Helga Balducci, Leslie Keir, Penny and Terry Davies, Tom and Joyce Stanwood, and Charlie and Paula Williamson. Your friendship means more to me than you can imagine. Dr. Hilly Bernard, the leader of another group, precursor of *The Joy of Being*, inspired a couple of the pieces in this book.

Many others have contributed to this intimate project by reading the manuscript or parts of it, teaching me to write better, coaching me, keeping my English (not my native language) in check and in many other ways. Dr. Rubén Ríos Ávila, Dr. Alice Weldon, Rev. Dr. José Norat Rodríguez, Rev. Dr. Carmen Gaud, and Rev. Ken Sehested offered invaluable and generous feedback on the manuscript. Rev. Michael Leuchtenberger, pastor of the Unitarian Universalist Church of Concord, NH, surprised me by reading one of my pieces during a worship service. And my deeply admired and respected friend and former colleague at the University of Puerto Rico, Dr. Luce López-Baralt, offered me such enthusiastic and generous feedback that my heart skipped several beats.

In the spring of 2019, I took a course on poetry and lyrical prose at the Great Smokies Writing Program of the University of North Carolina at Asheville. This five-week course, taught by renowned poet Jessica Jacobs, was one of the most significant and valuable learning experiences I have ever had. My limitless gratitude to my fellow students in this course, and especially to our extraordinary professor. Although I make no claims regarding Professor Jacobs' opinions of my writing, her influence has surely made this book better than it would have been otherwise.

Writing coach Tanya Whiton provided crucial and generous feedback on the manuscript, and I make the same caveat with her as with Jessica Jacobs. She made this book better than it would have been without her knowledgeable advice.

How could I ever repay Rev. Dr. Carter Heyward for her encouragement and the generous prologue of this book? She had already prologued my *The Holy Gospel of Uncertainty* (2017), and still enthusiastically accepted to do this one as well. It is an immense honor to be able to count on your authorized *imprimatur,* dear Carter!

Last but not least, my deep gratitude to the woman who has journeyed with me for over fifty years, whose steady love and generosity anchor my life, and who reads everything I write to make sure that I don't stray too far from the norms of the English language. Annie, you are my home.

INTRODUCTION

IT'S THE EIGHTH decade of my life, and my interest in the ways of the spirit reaches back to my earliest recollections of childhood.

Mass was incomprehensible, yet intriguing. The scent of incense, the statues of downcast or enraptured saints, the nasal, protracted singing of the congregation, all of it was boring and hypnotizing at once. Confession frightened me, but still I craved the forgiveness that made the Eucharist approachable.

Nuns! Why did they fascinate me? I was ten years old when I saw *The Nun's Story,* with Audrey Hepburn, and it held me spellbound. What about that film would appeal to a young boy? Why did the scene where Sister Luc lies on the floor of a church, arms spread in the form of a cross, touch me so?

Since those first religious experiences, my spiritual journey has followed many paths. I've been a Catholic, a Baptist, a Unitarian-Universalist, always with an undercurrent of doubt—now intense, now subdued—to the point where belief and disbelief have been an intertwining constant in my life. I've come to accept the tension between the two as the very grammar of my faith.

Science, the study of history and the insights afforded by the observation of nature and culture have been sources of both awe and skepticism. Whatever faith I may have, it does not allow me to dispense with the extraordinary discoveries of science; yet I question its competency when it comes to the unquantifiable, to all that remains unspoken after science does its calculations. It is perhaps the awareness of the immensity of my ignorance that makes me wary of ultimate conclusions. This is surely the reason why the reader will find many more questions than answers in the pages of this book.

The study of the past has confronted me with the history of suffering on this planet; suffering that does not abate, that endures today and will endure tomorrow, that never ceases to scandalize my faith. And in the observation of nature and culture I find both bliss and misery, glorious life and indifferent, meaningless death.

The reader will notice that the titles of eight of the book's pieces are presented in a slightly larger bold font and include indications of time. These pieces are intended to provide chronological markers, while the rest of the book, with its lack of a strict linear order, represents the ever-turning form of my spiritual journey.

I offer you, dear reader, this guileless haiku as an introit to the words of my book.

Its little eyes tightly shut,
tiny beak agape,
the nestling takes communion . . .

IN THE BEGINNING
(1953)

DOMINUS VOBISCUM, chanted the priest, and the people responded: *Et cum spiritu tuo.*

So began the tedious, impenetrable ritual that bored me Sunday after Sunday. The strange words, the chants—now standing, now sitting, now kneeling—the smoky scent that undulated in the air, the mantillas veiling the women's hair, the theatrical vestments of the priest. None of it made any sense. And yet, a heavy density filled the church that intimated questions I was too young to ponder.

One Sunday, my father took pity on me and offered a clue: "You know, son?" he said, "What really happens at mass is that the bread becomes the body of Christ, and the wine becomes his blood."

Padre Maximino *slowly turns to face the congregation and raises the consecrated host.* "Mysterium fidei," *he chants in a deep, echoing voice.*

Eyes wide-open, I anticipate the miracle, the lifting of the veil ... But the bread remains a white disk without halos or shimmering rays, absent any trace of flesh or blood.

And all I have to take home is that word, Mysterium, *to chew on through all the days of my life.*

Sensing Love

Both my kindergarten and first-grade teachers were mean old ladies who had never read Dr. Spock. To be fair, the Spanish translation of his celebrated parenting guide had not yet reached the shores of Puerto Rico. But, had they read it, I feel sure they would have dismissed his advice.

Mrs. Suárez, the kindergarten teacher, gave me an F on my very first homework because I followed her instructions to the letter. She wrote the number one on the blackboard, adding that it was just like a little stick, and told us to fill the first page of our notebooks with said number. So, I did. I filled the page with little sticks: standing sticks, prone sticks, diagonal, all kinds of little sticks.

At PTA meetings, Mrs. Boscana, my first-grade teacher, made us kiss her on the cheek in front of our parents and classmates. I'll never forget her cheek approaching my lips, the massive cheek covered in white face paint with a big red bullseye in the middle, all of it wrapped in a thick cloud of offending perfume.

These recollections make me think about children's uncanny capacity to sense love. Oh, you can easily fool them with things like the Tooth Fairy or the Three Kings, but not when it comes to knowing if they are truly loved. I had no doubt that both my grandmothers loved me; they didn't have to say it. But, surely, not my aunt Elba. And definitely not Mrs. Boscana.

So, I wonder, at what age do the nonverbal sensors that detect true love begin to break down?

MOLLY

ONCE IN A WHILE, Molly comes into my office, puts her paws on my knee and asks to climb onto my lap. I rarely deny her request. She falls asleep. To the rhythm of her breath, her cottony warmness against my paunch, I continue to work.

Or she doesn't sleep. Instead, she fixes her eyes on my face and stares, willing me to look down. For a moment, we gaze into each other's eyes as if across distant stars.

In fleeting instants of silent, mutual watchfulness, I glimpse the entanglement of our souls.

THE ONTOLOGICAL SIGNIFICANCE
OF BABY KISSES

SHE'S A KISSER. She generously blows kisses when we finish a Facetime session. In person she never shies away from a request for a kiss.

This little girl kisses almost everything, everything that she knows to love. She kisses her dolls, of course, and my dogs, and many of her toys. When she's ready to go to bed, she conducts a roll call, naming her dolls one by one and kissing them good night. She even kisses the walls of her home when she returns after a long day out! Kissing seems to be her way of bestowing realness on the objects of her affection.

Her kissing rites have brought to mind my own relationship with the things I loved as a child. My parents found themselves in a fix when they needed to buy new pillows. I refused to give up my old one and held on to it tightly. But they always won. The old pillow disappeared, and I cried myself to sleep wondering where my poor pillow now lived. The same happened when they traded in our old Plymouth for a new car. For my parents, the Plymouth was a thing that had lost its usefulness. For me, it was a being I loved, and usefulness had nothing to do with its worth.

When and why do children stop loving their old, torn baby blankets?

At what age do they lose the capacity to discern the soul of everything they love?

Where goes their ontological wisdom?

When does our magical world fold into a marketplace . . . into the cemetery of the expendable?

Who Were You? Who Are You?

WHEN I WAS A BOY, you were an old man with a white beard, yes. But you were strong and muscular, with biceps and triceps bigger than the Captain's, who had just come back from Korea. You were the scapular shield that kept me safe from *El Cuco* should he attempt to steal my soul by calling my name in the middle of the night, and even from *Correa Cotto*, on the lam and lurking behind bushes, razorblade in hand. You were a man, yes, but you had a womb that cradled me, and a beating heart that pumped red blood and fed me.

Then I was a boy, and you were my answer.

Today you are weak. You smile a lot, though, when you're a dandelion in bloom or the grin on my little Clara's face or the powdered milk that finally reaches the lips of a little boy in a Syrian camp. And you cry so much, too. Such a bleeding heart! Then, again, is there a way to stand vigil at any of the borders we have etched on the skin of the planet without weeping?

Now I am an old man. And you? You are my question . . . our bleeding wound.

LIFE WAS A PLACE

LIFE WAS A PLACE in the land of *Always Now*. Like a lake, its waters held within stable borders.

It was the place where we raced paper boats down the gutter under the rain, watched the boisterous truck of the garbage collectors pass, and listened for the trilling whistle that signaled the approach of the knife grinder.

It was the place where my grandmother's belly danced when she laughed, and where she dropped her teeth in a glass of water at night. The place where my teacher had red bull's-eyes on her cheeks. That's the way things were.

Then Time cast a spell, the dam was breached. And the waters of life rushed to flow downstream, always yonder.

HEARTACHE
(1956)

WHY WOULD AN EIGHT-YEAR-OLD boy ever need to worry about sin? Yet, when the teacher, in preparation for our first Holy Communion, described the sacrament of penance, I felt reprieved. It was as if in the very marrow of my bones there were terrible sins—perhaps from a previous life?—that would be finally rooted out.

Then she added: "But in order to be forgiven you must repent with *dolor de corazón*—true heartache—and resolve never to sin again."

How long does never last? How can I stow enough pain in my heart to last until the other side of never? Should I beat my chest like father during the mea culpa? *How many times a day?*

I'm sorry for lying to my mother, for telling her, out of jealousy, that Cano wanted to see Alene naked. But it's not only the lies. I'm a thief too. I stole Frankie's rubber horse, the one that looks so alive that I could almost hear it neigh and snort. It burned my hands, and it burned my pocket until I threw it back on Frankie's porch, and still it burns inside.

Oh, why do I sin? Why must I be so weak? Never is such a long, long time.

Rival Loyalties

In the schoolyard, surrounded by playing children, the boy opens his lunchbox to find a ham and cheese sandwich.

It's Friday. Lent. Useless to remove the ham. Surely the bread and the cheese were now tainted.

But his mom had made the sandwich for him, with her own hands . . .

In the schoolyard, the boy walks away from the laughter of children playing back to his classroom.

His heart beats in his mouth as he approaches the threshold, places a hand over the garbage bin and lets the sandwich slip.

A Little Nothing of a Flower

Have you ever seen a tiny weed pressing tendrils through the narrowest cleft in the asphalt?

Imagine how patiently, how assiduously the seed must exert itself in order to drive roots below and send a stem into the light. And then, once stabilized in such a hostile milieu, how resolutely, how tenaciously it must labor to push forth a flower, a little nothing of a yellow flower.

Tell me, little weed, how do you hold despair at bay?

THE PRIVILEGE OF HOPE

HIS LIPS SLIGHTLY PARTED in a hint of a smile, promises sparkling in his eyes, a mittened hand holding his cap in place against the blustery wind. The still image of this child, my grandson, embodies a legacy of memories, hopes, and dreams. Everything I am or have yet to be hovers over that smile and over those eyes brimming with the hopeful gaze of generations.

But how could I shield my hopefulness from the image of another boy whose body lolls on a beach? How could I look away from the dreams that crashed against that shore? How could I dismiss the apocalypse of his untimely death?

For everything that we are or have yet to be hovered over the body of that little boy in a red pullover and navy-blue shorts whose closed eyes can no longer brim with anything.

MAGIC SWORDS

THE NEIGHBORHOOD BUSTLES WITH a mix of accents and complexions, but the mellifluous tones of Dominican Spanish prevail above the din. The school is called Castle Bridge, and it is committed to bridging the distance that separates their mostly immigrant and minority students from a future to which they would ordinarily have no access.

The children welcome me, seem thrilled to meet their teacher's dad. "Would you like to ask him a question?", my son, José Daniel, suggests. And they jump into it with very little shyness. Mostly, they want to know what their teacher was like at their age.

José reads from Rick Riordan's *Percy Jackson and the Lightning Thief*, and I follow with the Spanish translation. A proper noun makes me stumble—*cortacorriente*—and a boy who had struck me as withdrawn volunteers a masterful explanation about a pen that turns into a magic sword. Stories about these children's lives come to mind: the all-too-common ordeals of families *without papers* and with worn-out hope.

Now they rehearse a scene from a play they're hoping to stage in a couple of months, *Zeus and Doubt,* a musical with rap lyrics composed by José. The main actor is absent today; an understudy takes his place. Probably short for his age, the boy has dark bags under his eyes that don't belong on the face of any child. He performs his memorized lines perfectly, with just the right diction and aplomb.

It is winter outside. And I yearn for spring and magic swords.

PRAYER

WINGS FLUTTERED IN my EARS as the priest planted the host on my tongue and branded my flesh. It was easy to pray then, a little boy talking to his papa: *Padre nuestro que estás en los cielos . . .* Sacred words that uncoiled effortlessly off my tongue reaching for his ears.

And then, much too soon, sin began to nibble at my flesh—venial, mortal, deadly—and prayer became a scapular that beat against my chest: *Mea culpa, mea culpa, mea maxima culpa.*

I reached the age of reason and doubt latched to my soul, feeding on the blood of trust, unveiling a landscape bereft of gods, pocked with the bodies of little children in red pullovers and navy-blue shorts lying still on an unwelcoming beach.

How could I possibly pray?

But I beg prayer to come back as I whisper: "Lord, I believe; help thou mine unbelief." (Mark 9:24)

AMADO

THE *IGLESIA BAUTISTA* SIÓN sat atop a hill in the *Quebrada Negrito* barrio of rural *Trujillo Alto*. It was a small, whitewashed, no-nonsense temple that housed a congregation of some one hundred members.

The church might be described as conservative, but not in the way this is typically understood. There was a deep respect for Scripture that was not quite literalism. And they had recently called a woman to be their pastor; one of the very first Baptist churches in Puerto Rico to see past Saint Paul's teachings on the role of women in the church.

There was a child, Amado, maybe twelve years old, who always walked to church alone. He moved with difficulty and had a severe language impairment. Didn't have much of a musical ear, but never missed on singing along with the congregation, loudly, often holding the hymnal upside down. And Amado always stood beside the pastor at the end of services to send the congregants off with a handshake and a broad smile of big, white, crooked teeth.

There was a singularity about the child that was rarely mentioned, and then only in whispers. Amado was neither a boy nor a girl. The mother, Aleja, had decided to raise the child as a boy, but people wondered what would happen at puberty. "What if he turns out to be a girl?" "What if he never reaches puberty?" "What if . . . ?"

One thing we knew for a fact: *Amado* is Spanish for *beloved*.

WHY NOT WHY?
(1954–1961)

"Literature begins with that 'why,' even if we were to answer that question over and over with an ordinary "I don't know.""

—OLGA TOKARCZUKS

EVERY WEEKDAY MORNING the aroma of roasting coffee poured out of the *Yaucono* mill, hovered briefly over *Fernández Juncos* Avenue, then rushed to spill over the schoolyard at *Academia Santa Mónica*. Sixty-six years later, the smell of roasting coffee still calls to mind the heavenly apparition I witnessed on my very first day of school.

She wore a long white dress and a funny sort of hat, from which hung a piece of white cloth that draped over her back. And a big chain of black beads dangled from her waist reaching almost the hem of her skirt. Had she been floating on a cloud with baby angels fluttering around her head, I wouldn't have been any more impressed.

What was under her clothes I could not begin to suspect. It could be anything: magic dust, heavenly cotton balls, who knows? Certainly not the body of an ordinary human being who—God forbid—pooped and peed.

I was instantly lovestruck.

As it turned out, some of the nuns at my school were too mean to be heavenly. But a few were gentle and kind. Like Sister Maura Patricia, whose smile and green eyes dispelled all fear and shyness.

It was Sister Maura who explained the origin of sin way back in the days of the Garden of Eden. She closed her lesson with these words: "And that is why, children, as the offspring of Adam and Eve, we are all born with the stain of sin on our souls."

"But why?" I asked, "It's not fair!"

Sister answered: "In matters of faith, we must never ask why."

"How come?" I replied.

And Sister laughed.

Sister, Sister, you're so pretty when you laugh, so beautiful in your unblemished white habit, immaculate like my soul yearns to be. And you smell so clean, like Argo starch and Castile soap.

You're my own Audrey Hepburn, my Sister Luc, and I quiver when I conjure you lying on cold stones, a fallen cross breathing sacred vows.

I trust you and I want to believe you. But, how come we should pay for Adam's sin back in the olden days? And why not "why," my favorite question?

And why would "I don't know" be a wrong answer?

What fear skulks in our hearts, Sister, that we should be embarrassed to not know, and turn mystery into taboo?

FORM

YOU MIGHT SAY the body of a flower is but an evolutionary ruse to fascinate nectar-sipping insects.

But why, I would ask, does it captivate *me*? Why do I relish the whorls of petals and sepals? Why does the nubile lip of this cattleya entice me so that I am seduced to venture up into the nuptial chamber and beg a kiss?

My Grandmother and the Universe

WHAT IS THE BRUSH of a kiss without skin to feel? What are the notes and rhythms of a Piazzolla tango without ears to hear? Where go the waves, the liquid mirrors of a Sorolla seascape, without eyes to see? What happens to our favorite book, the one we would read a hundred times, when there is no longer anyone to read?

When our words are no longer heard, no longer read, and no one remembers that my grandmother's skin felt like rice paper and smelled of truth, that she recalled the drills of nineteenth-century Spanish soldiers in the town square of *Vega Baja*, that her second child was stillborn; when no one remembers that she was sure to die on a Saturday, that well into her old age she was capable of wonder at the sight of a *reinita* building its nest in the *níspero* tree, that to sit by her, under the warmth of her presence, was deeply reassuring; when no one, absolutely no one recalls that there was in her a kindness that disallowed all cynicism, what then? Will she have existed at all?

What is the universe at last? A crisscross of waves longing for awareness?

Life Dances

Suppose that a succession of cinematographers were able to film the unhurried life of a *Ceiba pentandra* tree, from the thorny trunk of its decades-long youth, through the display of tabular roots that buttress the trunk like the stem of a chalice, to its mature, multi centenary girth.

Imagine the resulting film projected in superfast motion, so we're able to witness the wholeness of the *ceiba's* life in a couple of hours. Wouldn't we be awed before the astonishing choreography of a living tree?

Life dances. And all I want to know is why.

A Third Eye

"You know, papa? We have three eyes."

"Is that so?" asked your papa. "Where might that third eye be?"

"Inside our head, under the skin of our forehead!"

"And why would we need a third eye, an invisible one for that matter?"

"But, papa, that's how we see our dreams!"

How can you know this, my boy, at such a tender age? How can you know what Rumi knew in thirteenth-century Persia at the pinnacle of his wisdom?

That the body is a device to calculate the astronomy of the soul?

EVOLUTION

HAVE YOU SEEN a clock portraying the history of Earth in the span of a single day?

Life awakens at four in the morning, and it's already late afternoon before reproduction falls for the enticements of sex, late night before milk flows through the breasts of female mammals, and only near midnight do humans stand upright and are able to see the stars.

In those two or three minutes before midnight everything else has happened, and it was only seconds ago that we learned to speak. How many nanoseconds ago did our brains develop the capacity to hope and ponder?

How is it, then, that we feel authorized to come to conclusions? Who appointed us to reduce the splendor of the universe to the size of our infant minds? And, what if metaphysical inquiry is the wrong compass to search for God?

Why are we so impatient for certainty?

THE CREATION OF THE WORLD

I READ THIS SOMEWHERE: The spider spins silk out of her body, knits a web, turns around, and calls it world.

Not silk from our guts to create our world; instead, we knit webs of words and thought.

When our webs tear? We rush to weave a patch, stretch it tight over the chasm, turn around and whisper "Whew!"

It's in the Bible, how we cut down a tree, use the wood for kindling, save a piece, carve an idol and, forgetful, turn around and call it god.

A New World
(1967–1970)

The main entrance to the University of Puerto Rico leads directly to *La Torre*, the emblematic tower at the center of campus, an homage to Spanish architecture. As I walked toward the soaring structure on that very first day of classes, every step resounded in my chest, and I could hear the rustle of other invisible steps behind me, the strides of parents, grandparents and great-grandparents careful not to walk on my shadow on which they spilled the petals of ancestral hope.

When I stepped under the half arch of the tower, the doors of a new world opened to me. A world of queries and ideas that challenged almost everything I knew. A world that would lead me to question the certainties of kin and childhood.

No, the Americans did not arrive in 1898, like guileless pilgrims. They invaded and occupied.

Yes, James Joyce wrote the profane, lustful Ulysses *and not only the Dubliner stories granted entry into our sanitized Catholic anthology.*

And, yes, there are unimaginably remote black holes at the center of galaxies, so massive and so dense that nothing can escape their gravity, perhaps not even our prayers.

And, for all we know, politics might require the occasional killing of innocents, as Machiavelli argued. Which is perhaps why god is such a skillful politician.

That is, if god exists at all.

What if all the hunger in Bangladesh and the napalm in Vietnam and this damn drought that apportions sand rather than water down our faucets have nothing to do with myths or gods, and everything to do with us?

It can be dazzling this light that rushes in on the wings of mind-stretching ideas. It can be painful this piercing light, this inquisition of endless *hows* and *whys* committed to the erasure of faith and mystery.

I couldn't begin to suspect it then, but academia would become the landscape of my adult life. A landscape where I never felt totally at home. On the one hand I enjoyed the freedom of inquiry and the tradition of rigorous thought. On the other hand, I deplored the silliness and arrogance that can be found in university life.

I experienced academia as a strange land to whose citizenship I had no birthright.

Gift-delivering Waves

IMAGINE! A VAST SPECTRUM of electromagnetic waves weaves through the universe and we cannot see it.

Innumerable beams of varying wavelengths crisscross this room zigzagging through our bodies and we cannot perceive them.

Everything we see outside the window, the swaying branches of the pine trees against the blue sky, the bountiful shades of forest green, the early-rising yellow daffodils of spring or the pinkish-white summer blossoms of the mountain laurel; this and everything else we see or have seen or will see, everything that reaches our eyes, our brain, our understanding, rides on a miniscule band of the spectrum. To myriad other wavelengths we are blind.

Imagine! A sensory feast delivered on a tiny band of light; the pageant of a universe called into being just for us!

Imagine, as well, the bounties that might ride on the vast flow of motley light not meant for us.

WHO ARE WE?

WE ARE THE STORM whose name belies its nothingness.

We are flow made possible by time,
the stone that hides a quivering heart,
the bud that unfolds into a flower,
the lamb that wobbles on its limbs,
the baby learning to use her body,
the mother who strives to be a mother,
the old man unlearning to be a man.

We are dance whirling across the cosmos.

The Perils of Names

What if Adam and Eve lost paradise not because they sinned, but because they traded bliss for the power to name the world?

Beware the dangers of naming! I say "woman," and the opposite comes to mind: "man," an antonym that carves a thick trench where translucence would hold sway, where brawn and suppleness would run into each other like the hues of the sky at dusk.

I say "Puerto Rican," and maybe you hear echoes of West Side Story: *Puerto Rico, my heart's devotion . . .* Or maybe you mishear "Costa Rican," and the quetzal comes to mind. Or perhaps you even wonder how I crossed the Río Grande.

Naming casts an arresting light that hardens the focus of our gaze into a fenced-in object that can no longer be anything else. So, please, look into my eyes and resist the temptation to distill the multitudes in me into a single petrified name, and I will look into your eyes and try to see everything that you can be as long as you remain nameless.

What is Truth?

"A chorus of living wood sings to the woman: 'If your mind were only a slightly greener thing, we'd drown you in meaning.'"

—RICHARD POWERS

"MEANING IS CONTEXT BOUND, but context is boundless," declared Jonathan Culler, and his words have bedeviled me ever since I first read them. They portended an indisputable relativism, the impossibility of universal meaning.

All claims to meaning and truth are decipherable only in their context.

For any claim of truth there is a context: a complex web of ideas, values, experiences and perceptions that are inevitably grounded in a given standpoint. And the number of possible standpoints is endless.

No cultural, no spiritual, no moral precept can lay claim to universal truth.

Good news, if your viewpoint is moored in a colonial context: the empire's claims are based on power, not truth! But a treacherous gospel as well, because it would ultimately consign all arbitration of truth to power. *History is written by the winners . . .*

But one might ask: doesn't science have an unimpeachable claim to truth? Look closely, however, and you will realize that science is perhaps unassailable when calculating, but an incompetent arbiter of meaning.

What if language and argumentative reason are but the shadow life of truth and meaning? What if they are mirrors that inevitably distort the light they reflect? What if language and reason can only offer us a sorry approximation of what can never be said? And will we ever escape the need for interpretation?

What if truth is the scar that slithers across a battered woman's face?

Or the enfolding arms that shoo away the fear of a child?

The disfigured land where a forest has been razed?

Or even the hands of the old woman who seeds her garden every spring?

LOOKING FOR GOD

RULER IN HAND I set out in search of God. To no avail.

I exchanged the ruler for a magnifying glass, a microscope, then a telescope, but still there was no god to find.

Others, better equipped than I, trained sonars on the deepest oceans, radio telescopes on the edges of the universe, electron microscopes on the infinitesimal with equally futile results.

But, can the tendrils of kindness be perceived through the lens of a microscope, the flicker of joy through the eyepiece of a telescope? Can the hues of tenderness be sundered by a spectrograph? Can electrons in a vacuum tube ever trace the density of yearning?

Can any organ or instrument perceive the blinding clarity of love?

Disabused of my folly, I set out once again in search of God. Awe is my compass, and holy uncertainty my walking cane.

The Quieting of Questions
(1978–1983)

Now a married man with small children and an instructor of French at the University of Puerto Rico, we moved the family to the countryside in *Trujillo Alto*. I needed a counterbalance to my academic life, a life that I found fascinating and terrifying, a life that asked me to commit social class suicide in favor of more refined tastes and ever more penetrating thought.

The thick odor of loam and manure, the battle cries of the *pitirres* and the crimson hues of the *maga* flowers anchored me in the palpable truths of nature, while the bulls, bellowing like cargo ships, seemed to announce my arrival at port.

Not long after our move, we visited a small Baptist church just over the hill from our home. One Sunday morning, the pastor, one of the first women to be ordained by the denomination in Puerto Rico, called us to accept Jesus Christ as our personal Lord and Savior, and I hesitantly raised my hand.

"*The LORD is* in his holy temple. Let all the earth keep silence before him."

Silence, yes, silence! The stillness of dumbfounded trust, the shushing of the thousand questions! The soothing chords of redemption! The song of dazzling clarity that loops in my mind, over and over, like an earworm!

Rest, yes, rest from the puncturing pain of doubt! The all-encompassing serenity that sings lullabies in my core!

Joy, yes, joy! The utter delight of belief, the sedative joy of the thousand answers!

But the soothing effects of conversion did not last. Within two months, the killings at *Cerro Maravilla* took place. Two young *independentistas*, proponents of independence for Puerto Rico—one of them the stepson of a dear colleague—were ambushed and murdered by the police. This brutal crime shocked me out of all clarity and serenity.

Shortly thereafter, I enrolled at the Evangelical Seminary of Puerto Rico, an ecumenical institution with a tradition of serious scholarship. One thing I wanted from Seminary: that it answer my questions without deceit. If my faith was to endure, it could not be through artfulness or evasion.

I had come to the right place with respect to the absence of deception, but it was not the place for ultimate answers. If anything, the experience of seminary gave me depth, context and a vocabulary for more precise questions. The trial of Almighty God would continue, now quiescent, now surging, and I've never known for sure if I'm to be solicitor or prosecutor.

EMPATHY

A SIX-YEAR-OLD GIRL, nicely dressed, stands alone on a sidewalk in the city of Tbilisi, Republic of Georgia. Passersby stop to ask if she's lost, where her parents are, does she need help.

The same girl stands alone on the same sidewalk in the city of Tbilisi, Republic of Georgia. She wears shabby clothes and has smudges on her face. Nobody stops. Nobody asks anything. Nobody looks, nobody sees.

(Cut to a restaurant in the same city of Tbilisi.)

The girl, once again attractively dressed, enters the restaurant and approaches some tables. The strangers smile at her, ask questions, caress her cheek. One patron makes a paper boat for the girl to take home.

The same girl, poorly dressed, disheveled hair, enters the same restaurant and approaches several tables. One woman reaches for her purse and holds it tight on her lap. A man puts his hand on the girl's shoulder and points away. Another diner finally asks a waiter to show the girl to the door.

(Cut to the public library in Brevard, North Carolina.)

An older man sits alone at one of the reading tables. He is working on a homily about empathy and has just finished watching the video of the little girl in the city of Tbilisi. He wonders how anyone can be so heartless. "How can we be so attuned to the signifiers of social class that we fail to see the child behind the smudge? A little girl, for God's sake!"

34

The man raises his eyes as a stranger walks into the building. The stranger wears pink tights under multicolored clownish shorts and has pink hair. An earring dangles from the left ear.

"What the . . . ?" the man thinks. "How can anyone go out in public looking like that?" "Is it a woman or a . . . ?" is the man's last silent question before he cuts himself short.

Who I Am

I am no-one,
a tiny stitch in the fabric of the cosmos,
a wee nodule of awareness,
a galaxy of whirling particles.

I am no-body,
an inspirited sail of twirling molecules
fraught with the breath of creation.

I am no-thing,
not a stone but a breeze, a gale, a journey.

No-thing but a trace of dancing grace.

Movement

MURMURATIONS they call them,
clouds of starlings that sway in the sky,
so tight at times they merge into a dark bouncing ball.
So sinuous at other times
they dance in ecstatic flow.

Ah, their movement,
the choreography of a universe
intent on refuting meaninglessness
if only through the splendors of movement and form!

CLEVERNESS

THE BAYA WEAVER BIRD entwines its gourd-shaped nest in the *acacia* tree.

The honeybee waggle-dances atop the honeycomb to map the way to food.

The turtle hatchling, coaxed by invisible enticements, waits until dark, crawls its way through layers of sand, and wiggles out to sea.

The trees in a forest, fluent in the ancient tongue of chemicals, commune with each other.

Even the web of sounds and silences that is language, exquisitely tempered for meaning, a maze of nuance equally apt for revelation and dissimulation, an intricate fabrication that far exceeds the intelligence of any speaker.

Whence this dazzling cleverness that suffuses the universe?

CERTAINTY ENVY

I ENVY THE CERTAINTY of atheists, their talent for deduction, their subjugation of meaning to the authority of the empirical, and of God to the laws of probability.

I also envy the certainty of believers, their ability to trust, surrender questions, put all doubt to rest, and gloss over the perplexing gaps of experience.

Unlike them, I meander along a hazy path that twists and turns between faith and disbelief, now blinded by clarity, now by darkness, oftentimes dazzled into silence, dumbfounded by the abysmal depths of my unknowing.

ORTHOPRAXIS
(1983–1987)

AFTER SEMINARY, I went on to do a PhD in theology and literature at Emory University in Atlanta, where my family and I began to attend Oakhurst Baptist Church, a community of believers who have devoted themselves to a living gospel of compassion and justice. In the mid-eighties, they had a shelter for homeless men, welcomed LGBTQ believers into full communion, and had a female associate pastor, all badges of honor that would eventually earn them the expulsion from the Southern Baptist Convention.

My doctoral studies and the experience at Oakhurst exposed me to a faith that privileged orthopraxis over orthodoxy, which turned my theological questions on their head. My dissertation on Haitian literature afforded me an undissembling vista unto man-made evils that confounded all spiritual elucidations.

It was not God who needed to be on trial. Passages of Scripture coiled in my mind indicting *me* for not doing enough, not being enough: *Sell all you have and give it to the poor; Raise your knife against your beloved son; Hate your father and mother and wife and children if you want to follow me* . . .

I soon discovered myself unable, unwilling to meet the challenges of such a radical faith. But neither could I find refuge in any form of tranquilizing religiosity. I became one with the rich young ruler of the Gospel, sadly watching Christ traverse a widening, raging sea, while I sat on one of the last pews in church trying to beat the sin of privilege out of my chest.

A Door Between Chapels

I CARRY A CHAPEL in my heart where I light candles for this merciless, beloved world.

Candles for the scores of sea turtle hatchlings and seahorse fry, whose sole purpose in life is to be redundant.

Candles for the tigers, the pangolins, the gorillas, pressed against the firing wall of our voracity.

Candles for the children of *Jabalia, Katumba, Bidi Bidi,* whose only horizon is yet another wall of woeful tents.

Candles for the Angolan, the Syrian, the Salvadoran refugees, whose anonymous deaths seem algorithmically decreed by a distant god.

Candles for the vast, brushed aside remainder of an uncaring arithmetic.

Call me maudlin, gloomy, pessimistic. Urge me to open windows, to let in light. Tell me how mistaken I am to not see the beauty . . .

Oh, but I do see the beauty, the splendid beauty for which in my heart I carry a chapel as well. But, pray tell, is there a way to open a door between chapels?

The Law

It seems always to come after. After we are comfortably seated at the table. After we have seized the land, and the soil needs to be tilled. After we—immigrants of yesterday—are settled in today's comfort. It is then that we *know* Blacks to be less than whole, and immigrants of today, *bad hombres*.

It is then that we build the walls.

Safe in our privilege, we close the gates and weave stories in which we are the heroes and the keepers of a sacred Law.

CHRONICLERS

REMEMBER THE CLOSING MINUTES in the film *The Truman Show?* The scene where the eponymous character attempts to flee from his made-up world in a little sailboat? Remember how the boat's bow punctures the fake sky? What an overwhelming realization, to discover that even our cerulean horizon lies within the boundaries of a sham!

What if we are living in someone else's script?

What is our story about, torturing paradise into hell?

What lies beyond our deceptive horizons?

What manner of author scripted us to the point of language only to see us tear into the precious fabric of nature?

Were we fated to chronicle our own demise?

FINDING GOD

WE LIFTED OUR EYES to the heavens, and were mesmerized by the stars. Such vast, beckoning beauty must hold the key to all riddles.

Transfixed, we endeavored to win their favor. We chanted for them, whirled for them, beseeched them for answers.

Disheartened, we turned to rabbi Heschel and asked: "Why is it so difficult to find God?" And the rabbi answered: "Because you refuse to look low enough."

Centuries ago, a star had urged us to look away from the heavens. "Not out there!" it called, "not beyond the stars!" "Lower, lower, much lower!" it cried. Until it settled over a lowly trough.

Too lowly for our taste.

INTERIM
(1987–2007)

FROM 1987 TO 2007, my spiritual life was an ongoing struggle between faith and doubt, between trust and pessimism, action and passivity. I continued my relationship with the Baptists at the *Primera Iglesia Bautista de Caguas* in a now-earnest, now-lukewarm cycle, until I stopped attending church at some point in the early 2000s.

Early 1990s

Last Thursday, God spoke to me. I was driving home on the Caguas *expressway, the car crowded with guilt and anxiety, when I heard a voice: "Rest in me." Not an audible voice, like you hear on the radio, but an extrasensory voice, a soundless voice spoken by my mind but not of my mind. The relief was immediate. In an instant, all gloom fled.*

It didn't last. A couple of hours later I was doubting that it could really have been the voice of... what? God? Really? Tricks our minds play on us, a madness of sorts, soothing but not real.

Doña Iris comes to mind; my loveable, sweet friend. Without batting an eye, she can go from saying that the corn muffins are still warm to apprising you of what God told her that morning. Torn in two, I wonder how doña Iris will react when I tell her about last Thursday, while I ponder if this is how lunacy begins.

Our children began to phase into adulthood, so my wife and I decided to turn our plans for retirement into reality.

We settled in Brevard, a small town in Western North Carolina surrounded by a mountainous landscape of oak, hickory, sassafras, and hemlock forests crisscrossed by streams and waterfalls. And I began to feel renewed spiritual stirrings. We visited a number of churches, eventually opting for All Souls Cathedral, an Episcopal congregation, where we stayed for several months. But, as much as I enjoyed the beautiful liturgy that evoked my Catholic childhood, I found myself unable to recite the Creed with any form of conviction. Misgivings about certainty and doctrine, prevented me from participating with integrity in the sacramental life of the church.

Picoseconds

A PICOSECOND—one trillionth of a second—the duration of the first *era* after the Big Bang. Within this mystifying instant: stages, phases, epochs, so many *befores* and *afters*.

The bee hummingbird beats its wings eighty times in one second. How many cosmic eras pass between each beat of its wings?

How many millions of universes have burst into being in the eons since the word picosecond fluttered its wings before my eyes?

Unfathomable magnitudes

There are magnitudes for which our minds are unsuitable. Astronomical distances, for example, or the endless reams of information traversing cyberspace, or the scale of suffering on our planet.

I am reminded of the story of Saint Augustine and the angel. The learned theologian walked along the seashore pondering the mystery of God. He saw a little boy who walked again and again to the water, a shell in hand, filled the shell and emptied it into a hole in the sand. Approaching the child, Augustine asked what he was doing. The angel responded: "I am pouring the ocean into this hole."

The venerable sage laughed at the angel's expense. "Can't you see, my poor boy" he asked, "that the ocean will never fit into that measly hole?"

There are magnitudes for which our minds are holes in the sand. Picoseconds, for example, or the wealth of the one percent, or what we blithely call God.

Quid Pro Quo?

THESE ARE PANDEMIC DAYS that provoke apocalyptic imaginings. Around the world, thousands fall ill or die every day. Even the Amazon river, deep in the Brazilian jungle, has become a conveyor of death.

Our religious feelers are hypersensitized. Some suggest that we pray to the *Salus Populi Romani*, the image of the Virgin Mary reputed to have ended a plague in the sixth century. Others urge us to entreat the Crucifix of *San Marcello*, which seemingly ended another plague in the sixteenth century. Still others, trustful of the efficacy of collective supplication, invite us to join a global moment of prayer at a given time and day.

I understand the intention of these pious invitations—they bring people a measure of comfort in difficult times. But they make me wonder about the nature of our relationship with God. Is our God an omnipotent being who craves adulation?

I appreciate the solace that comes with this unquestioning faith, the relief of a *quid pro quo* that plainly names the price of our salvation, that allows us to believe that we will be spared the suffering that has been the daily bitter bread of this planet since the inception of life. But wouldn't our relationship with such a god be based on fear in the face of power?

There is no fear in love.
But perfect love drives out
fear, because fear has to do
with punishment. The one
who fears is not made perfect in love.
(I John 4:18).

To put it bluntly, how could I love a god who would spare our beloved children and grandchildren because we prayed in the right way, while ignoring the pleas of so many other mothers and fathers whose beloved daily drown in the Mediterranean or starve in Yemen, are abducted into prostitution or molested by a man of the cloth?

In the midst of his crucifixion, Jesus is believed to have uttered a heart-wrenching prayer: "My God, my God, why have You forsaken me?" Christian faith holds that this man who feels abandoned at the cross by God and Father is paradoxically the very incarnation of God. There is, thus, at the heart of this faith, the gift of a divine solidarity, of a God that denudes God's self of all *godness* and accompanies us into the entrails of suffering and death. Yes, there is Easter too in the Christian faith, but doesn't it come after the cross?

The God that I can worship—the God that I long for—loves us unconditionally and invites us to love back freely, without any transactional caveat, trusting not that we will be spared, but rather that suffering and death will not have the last word.

TELL ME

WHEN HAS NO one died for lack of care?
WHEN HAVE NO bodies lain by the side of a road?
When have no families been severed
at the crossroads of an ordinary day?
When has no immigrant crouched in the rubble,
squatted under dry fronds?
When have no children been orphaned by legal decree?
Yesterday or the day before yesterday or even the day before,
when did no one suffer the unspeakable amputation of a child?

Tell me.

When was it not the end of the world?

THE VIOLENCE OF MEANING

WORDS HAVE MEANING only in the framework of the language and culture to which they belong. Take the word *siminoco*, which you will not find in the dictionary of the Royal Spanish Academy. Its meaning unfurls only in a Puerto Rican context: an endlessly useful term to denote any object whose proper name the speaker does not know or is unable to remember. In any other context, the word is just a meaningless string of sounds.

Even the meaning of concepts that strike us as universal, like "man," only unfolds as a function of time and place. In the antebellum United States, a slave was deemed to be a fraction of a man. A bloody war was fought over rival understandings of this little word, and women have increasingly contested being subsumed under its rule.

The word "god" has a thousand meanings depending on who utters it, where and when. And the world is on fire over different understandings of who God is and what God stands for. What does the word mean when uttered by a fundamentalist Christian? When uttered by a Unitarian-Universalist minister? What does "god" mean in an ISIS camp? In a rustic church in the Amazon? In an Orthodox synagogue? What does this word mean when uttered by a white supremacist? What does it mean when whispered by a mystic?

So, I wonder, are we condemned, even in an increasingly globalized world, to endlessly fight each other over meaning and the consequences of meaning? Is meaning inseparable from conquest and repression? Will there ever be a global culture, and will global meaning always be arbitrated by those who control global resources? Must conflicting meanings always operate as acts of resistance or guerilla warfare?

Will it ever be possible to construct a world of universal compassion, kindness and tenderness? How would meaning be arbitrated in such a world?

INTIMATIONS OF DUSK
(2006–2020)

I BELIEVE it was in 2010 that we first attended a service at the Unitarian Universalists of Transylvania County. This church, located in Brevard, North Carolina, coheres not around dogmas, but rather around principles to which I could give assent without dissimulation or duplicity. It is a community of fellow seekers with diverse religious backgrounds and spiritual urgencies whose fingerprints can be found in every single local initiative related to justice, peace and love for our fellow human beings and for the planet.

At UUTC we found a mature spiritual community whose first and foremost principle is the inherent worth and dignity of every person. "Whoever you are," affirms our pastor every Sunday, "whomever you vote for, whomever you love, whatever your religious background, if any, you are welcome here."

GETTING OLD

WOULDN'T IT BE NICE if aging, on its own, would prepare us for being old? It doesn't. Looks like, as with every other stage of life, if there is a way to learn oldness it's only by being old.

I hear the rebukes of so many who don't like to face the aging process. "Oh, don't be such a killjoy," they are prompt to cry, "age is just a number. All that matters is how we feel." "Well, that's even worse," I riposte, "I feel terrible!"

I evoke the old people I've known throughout my life wondering if they might serve me as models. But I soon discover that there's an inevitable link between the ages of our life. It appears that we can only be the kind of senior that our previous ages have cooked. By the time we're old, it's too late to change the recipe.

Then I wonder if there's some genetic preordination to the old person we become. If there is, mine surely does not come from my father. He passed away within weeks of his eighty-fourth birthday, astonished that he was actually dying without ever being old. No, if I am to inherit my oldness it would have to be from my mother who died at ninety-five, deeply confounded by dementia, bless her heart. It seems to run in her side of the family. Both of her siblings and their father were long-gone by the time they passed away.

When I don't remember what happened on a previous episode of *The Plot Against America*, and my wife recounts it for me in lavish detail, I immediately think of my mom. When a friend from high school reminds me of how Mrs. Figueroa taught *El Quijote,* while I only remember that she did, my mom comes to mind.

When a word —as is too often the case— stubbornly refuses to visit my mind, I remember my mom.

It's just terrible how I catch myself spying on my mother in everything I do.

Is this it? I ask myself. Is this the beginning of the end? Will my mind simply fade away to the point where all questions will be forgotten, and any answer will be in vain?

After the Chrysalis

OXYGEN FILLS OUR LUNGS as we join the chorus of breath, the groaning chorus of labor pains that is this living planet.

The eclosion begins. The laborious nativity of a human being.

So much to see, to hear, to smell, to taste, to feel. So much to ponder in a single lifespan.

If we're blessed and wisdom has brushed our heart. If we've grasped that tenderness is the language of the Spirit. If we're fortunate and death is not oblivion. Might we be ready, on our deathbed, to leave the chrysalis? Might we be ready to gather in our arms all the wisdom and love we've known and carry them tenderly like a consecrated host?

Will we be ready to begin?

Have We Cancelled Their Future?

It feels like the end is nigh, doesn't it? Like the Earth has had enough of the daily, intimate violence inflicted on her. Like she's ready to spew the poison we have sowed on her skin and in her bowels. Like we've looted her mineral blood to the end of patience.

The orbit of time passes again by the dense shadow of death-worship. A centripetal, somber force threatens to swallow compassion, empathy, and tenderness.

And the goose steps of hatred parade once again under the light of noon.

I look into my grandchildren's unclouded eyes and trust looks back at me. Curiosity, joy, innocence look back at me.

My heart weighs on my chest like a brittle stone.

I think of the world where my grandchildren's lives will unfold. Uncertain about the efficacy of prayer, I pray for them still. But I wonder: have we cancelled their future?

Declaration

WORDS GET TIRED, don't they? Take the word "god," uttered with such contrary and jarring intents that it seems fatigued, useless, worse yet, banal. Hear then my declaration, my locked-in standard for this weary, wounded word.

Whatever the Bible says, whatever the Quran, whatever the Talmud, whatever the priest or the rabbi or the pastor or the imam or the guru or any would-be sage, God is love and only tender love.

If it is cruel, it is not God.

If it is hateful, it is not God.

If it is indifferent or dispassionate, if it injures or wounds, if it calls for blood or revenge, if it pits you against your brother or your sister or your neighbor, against Latinos crossing the border, Africans traversing the sea, Muslims begging for refuge, against those who cannot find themselves within boundaries imposed, if it calls a crusade or a pogrom or an intifada, if it urges you to see yourself or your family or your tribe or your nation as the measure of worthiness and suitability and belovedness, it is not God.

It is not God.

It is not God.

THE STAR OF KINDNESS

IT HAS BEEN SO LONG since faith consoled me.

As a child, beliefs, piously received like a consecrated host, sheltered me from the terrors and injustices of a child's life: my Motsy banished because he barked too much. Bullies. The fact of my parents' unavoidable death.

As a man, impelled by reason, I've let go of all doctrine, all illusion of seizing the eternal. I've wandered through territory where faith, a mirage, vanishes again and again, leaving me to dwell in makeshift tents.

A philosopher tells me, "There's no such thing as evil or good. They're just aesthetic mindsets." A child, a man, I rebel. I won't concede that the difference between tenderness and cruelty is arbitrary. That a gentle caress is not radically different from a cruel blow. That love is not truth.

I reset my compass to the star of kindness, and I journey on.

KYRIE ELEISON

"We eventually have to 'eat' the truth
rather than ever understand it."

—RICHARD ROHR

THESE ARE THE LATTER DAYS of my life, and you have yet to run out of a future for me. At every turn you have whispered, "You are enough!" And still, I continue to seek for shelter from your voice.

I have tried to flee from not understanding, from the never-ending questions that eviscerate me without the charity of a single answer.

I have tried to hide from your unrelenting love that places on my shoulders the unmet challenge of a reciprocating life. And still you whisper, "You are enough."

I have tried to flee from suffering, from the odds —perish the thought— that you might ask me to place my child on a sacrificial altar in the land of Moriah. But also, from the countless sorrows that can be witnessed on the face of just one starving boy or girl begging for refuge across a cruel border. And still you whisper, "You are enough."

Who am I that you should be mindful of me?

I have wanted to see with your eyes, but you touched my near-sighted eyes and said, "You are enough."

I have wanted to weave a theology of everything, a coherent, all-inclusive account of you. And, upon my failure, you have whispered, "You are enough."

I am a melody of disremembered notes that only you, in your infinite mercy, are able to sing.

And all I can reply is, "You, ineffable synonym of love and beauty and tenderness, you alone are whole!"

The fading image of a white disc, bereft of halos and shimmering rays, reenters my mind, and that old word, *Mystérium*, the same and yet so different, echoes in the chapels of my soul.

Eyes tightly shut, I lift my hands chanting *Kyrie Eléison!* as I receive you on my tongue.

Made in the USA
Middletown, DE
29 November 2021